THE *Cyclic God* HYPOTHESIS

WHY AND HOW GOD EXPERIENCES THE UNIVERSE THROUGH YOU:

A Brief Introduction to General and Special Scientific Panentheism

BALBOA
PRESS
A DIVISION OF HAY HOUSE

Dr. Michael F. Bohley, Th.D.

Balboa Press books may be ordered through booksellers or by contacting:

Balboa Press
A Division of Hay House
1663 Liberty Drive
Bloomington, IN 47403
www.balboapress.com
1-(877) 407-4847.

Because of the dynamic nature of the Internet, any web addresses or links contained in this book may have changed since publication and may no longer be valid. The views expressed in this work are solely those of the author and do not necessarily reflect the views of the publisher, and the publisher hereby disclaims any responsibility for them.

The author of this book does not dispense medical advice or prescribe the use of any technique as a form of treatment for physical, emotional, or medical problems without the advice of a physician, either directly or indirectly. The intent of the author is only to offer information of a general nature to help you in your quest for emotional and spiritual well-being. In the event you use any of the information in this book for yourself, which is your constitutional right, the author and the publisher assume no responsibility for your actions.

Any people depicted in stock imagery provided by Thinkstock are models, and such images are being used for illustrative purposes only.
Certain stock imagery © Thinkstock.

Printed in the United States of America

ISBN: 978-1-4525-6890-4 (sc)
ISBN: 978-1-4525-6892-8 (hc)
ISBN: 978-1-4525-6891-1 (e)

Library of Congress Control Number: 2013902782

Balboa Press rev. date: 03/13/2013

This book is for anyone who desires a sensitive and intelligent exploration of the intricacies and possibilities of their faith in God. Through reading it, one can be guaranteed a deeper relation to what it means to be human in our vast universe. A brilliant achievement!

– Colleen Kinney

For me, *The Cyclic God Hypothesis* connects science and God very clearly and methodically. I strongly recommend this read to anyone searching for answers to the whole deal! CGH is a logical analysis of how the Universe was created by God and how science fits into the larger puzzle. Please read and enjoy this masterwork. Thanks, Mike!

– Bill Stromberg

Standing upon the shoulders of giants, such as the philosophical likes of Whitehead and the process theologies of Cobb and Fox, Michael Bohley introduces us to a new phase in the genre of science and religion. He presents us with a refreshingly new dynamic of *panentheism*, the conception of God as being both transcendent (*God is more than everything*) and immanent (*God is in everything*). But unlike systematic theologian Paul Tillich, whose understanding of this dualism is based on an ontological development of the doctrine of God as Ultimate Reality, Bohley builds his case for "scientific" panentheism on the worlds of Physics and Astrophysics. Relying heavily on Gamow's (and Alpher's) "Big Bang" theory of the universe and the resulting "pulsating" aspect of ongoing expansion and contraction, he conceptualizes a "Scientific Panentheism" identified as the *Cyclic God Hypothesis*. One can only hope that this is but the first in a series of texts which continue to explore the myriad of issues concerning absolute truth vs. relativism; free will vs. determinism; or in traditional Christian terminology, doctrines regarding salvation, predestination and/or free will and choice. Based on his CGH, we begin to experience a *"Theophysics"* for the future, a "unified field theory" which incorporates within its metabelief structure all complementary beliefs. It is ultimately about "process" and evolving through and toward universal consciousness.

– The Very Rev. Paul E. Mottl, *Dean*
Providence Theological School

DEDICATED TO:

My theological, mystical, and scientific mentors: Messiah Yeshua, Apostle Paul, Apostle John, Dr. Albert Einstein, Dr. Carlos Castaneda, Dr. John C. Lilly, Dr. Fritjof Capra, and many other brilliant men and women too numerous to count. I am deeply grateful.

My soulmate, Colleen, without whom my time in the world (and God's experiences through me) would have been without the deepest form of *Eros.*

And to the greatest and most talented rock group of all time, *Yes,* who have been an inspiration to me since I was introduced to their masterworks, *Fragile* and *Close to the Edge,* as an eighteen-year-old freshman at Cornell University.

FOREWORD

I MAGINE, IF YOU WILL, AN ancient starry night. A being observes the vastness of the night sky while listening to the powerful force of the ocean waves on a nearby beach. The observer cannot help but feel separate from that which is being observed. It is vast, powerful and endless. By comparison, this one small being is powerless, finite and insignificant. Questions arise as to the meaning and purpose of the life of the observer. What is the purpose of being alive?

Imagine the passing of time and with it the increasing intelligence of beings on this planet. The need to answer questions surrounding the very nature of existence grows exponentially, as does the sophistication of the investigative process. Initially, images are painted onto cave walls telling stories of creation and beyond. Later, great institutions develop philosophical, scientific and theological disciplines. Great thinkers spend lifetimes examining examination itself. Scientific law, religious truths, and dogma become established beliefs in spite of the relatively limited understanding and knowledge of the totality of reality.

Imagine the passing of century upon century. A sense of separation from *all that is* grows concurrently with the divisiveness of the great religions and institutions. Contempt for other's beliefs, color, culture and ethnicity grows and begets war upon war—more and more separation.

Imagine the current day experience of human beings who are evolving spiritually and who seek to look deeper into the nature of the universe, stepping beyond the limiting confines of any one religion, theological concept, or scientific law. Imagine a brave and provocative investigation into the reality of God that brings into account ancient wisdom, sacred world texts and scientific inquiry to probe the questions surrounding existence itself. Imagine a theological reevaluation that brings us to a place of wholeness—no longer separate but totally connected and at one with our Creator and thus each other.

Bohley invites the reader to join him on such an adventurous journey. *The Cyclic God Hypothesis* provides a lens through which to look anew at the age old questions regarding how we came to exist, who and what God is, who we are and why we are here. The reader is wise to maintain an open mind and an open heart to grow ever closer to the manifestation of the divine within and without all of existence. We are left with the realization that there is a unity in all of creation that can only be spoken of in a single word – "one." Imagine.

Rev. Barbara S. Eberle, MA, OMC

Founder, Peace of God Chapel and Seminary

(The Peace of God Chapel and Seminary is a nonprofit organization providing a bridge for spiritual harmony through the compassionate understanding and tolerance among the faiths, cultures, and creeds in our world.)

TABLE OF CONTENTS

PROLOGUE

THIS IS AN INTRODUCTORY WORK on a metabelief system I call *General and Special Scientific Panentheism*. It investigates ways of thinking about God and the universe that can enhance both our intellectual understanding and our spiritual progress. As we proceed, we will consider ideas from mysticism, quantum physics, belief dynamics, and a variety of other subjects which will assist us in formulating our basic thesis. The metabelief system is also called *The Cyclic God Hypothesis,* for reasons that will become clear as we proceed.

The Cyclic God Hypothesis recognizes that God possesses both transcendent and immanent aspects or modes, and that an exploration of these complementary functions will lead to surprising new understandings of the nature of the Creator and the material universe. Some of the ideas explored in this book are ancient, and some are relatively new, but the particular synthesis of the various components is, to the best of my knowledge, original.

We will explore the structure of the physical universe, the nature of human consciousness, and the critical role of beliefs and belief systems in creating our personal realities. This exploration will provide a foundation for comprehending the core beliefs of *all* particular religious faiths (including Scientism) and is intended to precipitate a spiritual epiphany in the reader. This epiphany will enhance the reader's knowledge and instill a sense of wonder at the beauty, magnificence and complexity of God's creation.

We will also be seeking to answer the great questions of human existence: who are we, where did we come from, and why are we here? The answers I offer will require open-minded thoughtfulness on the part of the reader. I believe that the end result will be a sense of déjà vu, in which the reader will begin to remember what he or she already knows about God, self and the universe.

We are all part scientist and part theologian. It is no longer necessary to separate these two aspects of our personalities. We can realize that these seemingly disparate realities are simply complementary functions of the two hemispheres of our brains, and it is time that the hemispheres were integrated. In this book, I will put forth a view of science and religion which will result in a harmonious confluence of these two approaches to knowledge. It's time that we cease compartmentalizing our information about the universe and the place of the Creator and ourselves in that universe, and to recognize that the essential insights of religion and science are not and cannot be in conflict with one another. That which is true cannot conflict with any other truth. So we will explore science and religion by sorting the truth from received "knowledge" which may be true only for the moment. We'll do so by using logical analysis, intuition, and holistic synthesis.

We'll be gathering information from quantum physics to illuminate the path that lies before us, and we'll be utilizing information from allied disciplines to bolster our understanding of the structure and function of the physical universe and the consciousness which pervades and sustains it.

I'd like to disclose at this point that I am not a professional physicist or a professional theologian. I am simply a curious person who thinks about the world around him and tries to understand its structure, function, and purpose. Being fifty-three years old at the time of this writing, I have spent a significant amount of time thinking about how the universe came into being and what its purpose may be. The outlines of the Cyclic God Hypothesis as a metabelief system date from my late teens while a student at Cornell University, but relatively simple precursors of some of the components came to me much earlier, at about age nine or ten. Professionally, however, I am a counselor and chaplain. Though I am currently medically retired, I have spent many years dealing with clients' substance abuse issues and psychological problems, along with their spiritual conflicts and religious confusion. Since retiring, I have done volunteer counseling in church and halfway house settings. My counseling experience has encouraged me to contemplate the nature and function of the human mind and soul, and this thinking has led to the writing of this book.

Though I will speak of God in the masculine gender, please understand that this is simply a reflection of the Judeo-Christian tradition in which I was raised. I believe that God has no gender, but I prefer not to use the term It to refer to the Creator. Please substitute whatever term allows you to benefit from the ideas presented in this book.

1 – In The Beginning...

IN THE BEGINNING WAS GOD. God was all there was, and God remembered no beginning and could envision no end to himself.

God began to recognize a feeling within himself, and he called this feeling loneliness. This was an uncomfortable feeling, and God began to ponder ways in which he could be free of this feeling.

God opened a space within himself and, within the midst of this space, he spoke a Word. An explosion took place, and we call this explosion The Big Bang. Thus began the universe as we know it. This universe is contained within the bubble which God opened within himself. We will call it a reality bubble. It is possible that there are other reality bubbles, but we are aware of only this one. In the future, we may be able to discover whether or not other reality bubbles exist, other universes like or unlike our own, but for now we will content ourselves with exploring our own.

God infused the space within himself with matter/energy and with part of his own consciousness. That part of his consciousness which is within the reality bubble, we call the Immanent Godhead. That part which is without, we call the Transcendent Godhead.

As the matter/energy exploded outward from the center of the bubble God had created within himself, consciousness went with it. Matter/energy fused with space and became what I call the spacetime matrix. The spacetime matrix, or matrix for short, is pervaded with the consciousness of the Immanent Godhead.

Some physicists have realized that subatomic particles have an elementary form of consciousness, but most have not. This is entirely understandable, since science as a whole has not known what to do with consciousness during the entirety of its brief life. Science has, for the most part, chosen to believe that mind and matter are two entirely different things and that scientists must restrict their research to the material world. This, of course, has only delayed the inevitable. For centuries, consciousness was relegated to theologians and, more recently, psychologists. The study of the so-called hard sciences such as physics and chemistry was reserved for those intellectuals who had no interest in the messiness of the human psyche or God.

This was not always the case. Many of the great early scientists such as Isaac Newton were devoutly religious and were attempting to discover the laws of the natural world *as created by God.* Newton is regarded as one of the two greatest scientists in the history of science, the second being Albert Einstein. Einstein also believed in God, though he believed that God had created the universe and then stepped away, allowing it to progress according to the laws he had incorporated into it. This is a form of Deism and is a *partial truth*. It seems that most modern scientists, however, and physicists especially, are either atheists or agnostics. Some are vehemently opposed to any suggestion that God even exists, let alone that he created the universe or has an ongoing relationship with it. We will see, however, that theists, atheists and agnostics all have a place in God's world.

2 – THE FABRIC OF THE UNIVERSE

THE FABRIC OF THE UNIVERSE is the spacetime matrix. Matter/energy and spacetime intertwine to create this elementary matrix. The matrix is discrete or *discontinuous* due to its particle nature. This is what makes spacetime a quantum process. This quantum process is associated with consciousness, however, and is therefore also *continuous*. In his book *The Dancing Wu Li Masters* (2007), Gary Zukav quotes physicist E.H. Walker as follows: "Consciousness may be associated with all quantum mechanical processes...since everything that occurs is ultimately the result of one or more quantum mechanical events, the universe is *inhabited* by an almost unlimited number of rather discrete, conscious, usually non-thinking entities that are responsible for the detailed working of the universe." These "entities" are the subatomic particles which comprise the quantum (or energic) flux. Since matter *is* energy, the quantum flux plus

Einstein's spacetime continuum comprises the spacetime matrix, *along with* the Immanent Godhead.

Matrix theory can be classified as a quantum field theory. The matrix as a whole is the primary quantum field which is comprised of all lesser fields. Many of our comments about the spacetime matrix can be derived from the ramifications of a quote by the father of quantum theory, physicist Max Planck. He is quoted by author Gregg Braden in *The Divine Matrix* as follows: "All matter originates and exists only by virtue of a force... We must assume behind this force the existence of a conscious and intelligent Mind. This Mind is the matrix of all matter (Braden, 2007)."

Though I decided on the use of the term *matrix* before becoming aware of Braden's book and this quote from Planck, I was happy to find confirmation that others shared at least some of the conceptualizations which comprise the Cyclic God Hypothesis. As we continue, we will discover concepts from many other individuals which support our thesis. Some of these individuals are well known and highly respected scientists, and some are mystics. The reader may perhaps be surprised (and potentially pleased) to hear that I'll be quoting mystics. Atheistic scientists would be appalled by any suggestion that mysticism is a necessary tool for any fully formed understanding of the universe. Mysticism, as defined by *Webster's New World Dictionary*, is the "belief in the possibility of attaining direct communion with God or knowledge of spiritual truths, as by meditation." It is the *process* of attaining that knowledge, *the knowledge itself* and the actual *state of communion*. Anyone who has read Dr. Fritjof Capra's *The Tao of Physics* (1999) is aware of the similarities between descriptions of the mystical experience and concepts of quantum physics.

I would define mysticism as the process of, and knowledge obtained by, direct contact between a *focal manifestation* of the Immanent Godhead and the Transcendent Godhead. This contact brings *reminders of who we really are.*

Returning now to Gregg Braden's book, *The Divine Matrix*, we find intriguing comments by the author concerning his definition of the Matrix, as follows: "There is a field of energy that connects all of creation. This field plays the role of a container, a bridge, and a mirror for the beliefs within us. The field is nonlocal and holographic. Every part of it is connected to every other, and each piece mirrors the whole on a smaller scale. We communicate with the field through the language of emotion (2007)."

Upon reading Braden's account of the qualities of his Divine Matrix, I almost concluded that *The Cyclic God Hypothesis* did not need to be written. As I continued through the book, however, I realized that he was addressing a different set of issues related to the matrix: namely, how to access the matrix for healing. I, on the other hand, am addressing the origin, structure and development of the matrix as it relates to the motives of the Godhead.

And there are differences in our conception of the matrix itself. Therefore, I decided to write this book. I'd begun to research topics such as relativity theory, quantum theory and mysticism in 2002, when I began to write down my ideas about the Cyclic God Hypothesis. The outline of the theory had taken form when I was an eighteen year old freshman at Cornell University. I'd had minimal contact with formal works on religion, philosophy and physics at that time. I *had had* extensive contact with science fiction works since age twelve *and* I'd had a profound "mystical" experience of unitive consciousness while discussing the problem of human perception with a friend while a sophomore at Cornell.

That experience provided proof for me that we were all part of one organism and led immediately to the writing of a book of mystical poetry entitled *Forty-Two Fragments of Universe.* The Cyclic God concept informed the poetry.

By the time I'd finished writing *Forty-Two Fragments,* my desire to write about the Cyclic God ideas had been temporarily satiated. I did, however, take note of confirmatory experiences and readings over the ensuing years leading up to 2002, when I finally decided to write a book on the fleshed out version of my concepts. That notebook was lost. I began the process anew in July of 2007. The fabric of my personal universe has become the fabric of this book.

3 – The Cyclic God Hypothesis

IN THIS CHAPTER I WILL give an outline of two different versions of the Cyclic God Hypothesis. One is a *free will scenario* and the second is a *deterministic scenario*. This will allow the reader to more readily understand the points I'll be making as we proceed through the book. In this chapter I'll be going into detail about the physical processes involved. In this and subsequent chapters I will be quoting from the books found in my bibliography, all of which are excellent and highly recommended. Those quotes will clarify the quantum theoretical background for understanding CGH in detail.

As stated previously, God made a decision to open a space within himself and to create the physical universe within that space. This is another of the many ideas which I formulated on my own, only to discover later that it has precursors. In this case, the first formulation of the idea that I've been able to discover comes from the history of

Jewish mysticism, specifically the Kabbalah, as interpreted by Isaac Luria centuries ago. This may be an example of the independent development of similar ideas as a result of intuition into the actual state of the Transcendent Godhead, given that Luria was *also* a mystic. That, of course, is why core mystical ideas (*gnostic concepts)* are nearly identical across centuries and cultures. The Transcendent Godhead has allowed us to reach out to him and discover his personality.

The Big Bang occurs and matter/energy explodes outward in all directions from the center of the reality bubble. As the universe cools, atoms and molecules form. Clouds of gas form galaxies and solar systems within those galaxies. Solar systems are typically composed of stars, planets and moons. Ours also has an asteroid belt (possibly a destroyed planet). Galaxies form clusters and super-clusters. As planets cool, some generate life. I choose to believe that life is formed according to the instructions of the Creator, the Transcendent Godhead. This could take place in a number of different ways, and I will be presenting my opinion concerning the most probable means of achieving that end as we progress.

It is obvious, of course, that *no one really knows* what took place all of those eons ago. Common sense tells us that we rarely know with any certainty what took place last year, let alone decades, centuries, millennia, or billions of years ago. Specialists in any given scientific discipline are simply giving us their best educated *guesses* about how the universe, our particular world, and any given process in our world developed. And I will give you *my* guesses, bolstered by speculations from scientific and mystical specialists.

In scenario one, the *free will scenario,* and not necessarily at the very beginning of the physical process, consciousness in a limited form flowed into the creation. I believe that physicist E. H. Walker is right in stating that subatomic particles have rudimentary consciousness. In this free will scenario, matter/energy is conscious, though not necessarily self-conscious.

These focal manifestations (condensed, limited forms of the Immanent Godhead or Universal Consciousness) move through the spacetime matrix, *having experiences for God.* In fact, *the purpose of all focal manifestations (FMs) is to alleviate God's loneliness by having experiences for God.* You are one of the billions of ways in which God can have a human experience. Lest I be accused of heresy, let me point out that the Jewish and Christian Bibles, along with the Koran and probably numerous other primary religious texts, state that humans are made *in God's image.* This necessitates the conclusion that God has thoughts, emotions and behaviors. This may seem to be stating the obvious, but the obvious sometimes (oddly) needs to be stated. If nothing else, it brings these facts to immediate consciousness. It should also be noted that God needs to empty himself of the qualities which manifest his transcendent essence, namely omniscience, omnipotence and omnipresence, in order to take on the qualities of a focal manifestation. This is, of course, a voluntary process initiated specifically in order to have experiences which he could not have had while in the Transcendent state.

I should state that I choose to follow traditionalist Christian faith. This is the belief system with which I am most comfortable. It is one of a great many basic religious belief systems currently available on this planet. All of these systems are examples of *Special Scientific Panentheism.* In the *evangelical* Christian belief system (with which I have some disagreements), Jesus of Nazareth, called the Christ or Messiah (anointed one), is believed to be the one and only Son of God. But Jesus was situated in specific spacetime coordinates (was not omnipresent), admitted that he did not know everything that God the Father knew (was not omniscient), and gave no evidence of omnipotence (was sometimes unable to achieve mighty works – Matthew 13:57-58). The Bible tells us that God (the Father, the Transcendent Godhead) had *emptied* himself (Philippians 2:6-8) in order to be the Christ. In the Christian belief system, we are said to be brothers and sisters of Christ *and* sons and daughters of God. To me it is obvious that this is so because the Transcendent Godhead *emptied himself in order to become ALL focal manifestations* (conscious beings), including Jesus. In relation to the Cyclic God Hypothesis, we would say that God infused part of himself into the spacetime matrix (the creation), thus limiting himself and rendering himself capable of having an almost infinite number of experiences which were unavailable to him as the Transcendent Godhead.

All of these experiences are associated with the lives of FMs (focal manifestations) located within our known universe or reality bubble. All of the focal manifestations (humans, dolphins, sea horses, planets, stars, molecules, etc.) are located at a series of specific quantum spacetime coordinates. All are therefore finite. In CGH-1, the first Cyclic God Hypothesis scenario, these FMs live in a truly dynamic universe. This is a result of the fact that the physical universe is evolving in time and consciousness is moving out into space with all of the matter/energy. The matter/energy field entwines with space over time as the universe evolves.

Newton intuited God's creation of the spacetime matrix without intuiting the purpose of that creation. Dr. Capra captures this insight in the following quote from Newton's magnum opus, *Philosophiae Naturalis Principia Mathematica*: "It seems probable to me that God in the beginning formed matter in solid, movable particles, of such sizes and figures, and with such other properties, and in such proportions to space, as most conduced to the end for which he formed them (Newton, 1687)."

Newton was aware or believed that God created the physical universe, unlike many atheistic or agnostic "modern" scientists, but was unable or unwilling to deduce the true purpose of the matrix. This purpose is to be found in the motives of the Transcendent Godhead itself, and therefore does not vary with differences in belief among FMs within the matrix. In other words, *some things do not change no matter what we believe about them.* This will figure importantly in our forthcoming discussions about beliefs, metabeliefs, and the function of the spacetime matrix. Let it suffice to say at this point that many things within our reality bubble *do* change with changes in belief. The existence and function of the spacetime matrix does not change.

You will recall that the matrix is comprised of the quantum flux (which is an ocean of conscious energy particles) and the spacetime continuum.

The matrix possesses the quality of being discontinuous in its particle nature and continuous in its field nature. This continuity is a result of the presence of the consciousness of the Immanent Godhead.

The waves of the electromagnetic spectrum are made possible by this continuous ocean of particles which pervades all space and entwines with it. *There is no "empty" space!*

Support for this view comes from Einstein himself. Though he had done away with the concept of the ether in his 1905 paper on Special Relativity, he realized after completing his 1915 paper on General Relativity that the gravitational potentials in that theory served as a medium which could transmit disturbances through "empty" space. Walter Isaacson, in his definitive biography of Einstein published this year (2007), quotes Einstein from a lecture given in Leiden in 1920 as follows: "We may assume the existence of an ether. To deny the ether is ultimately to assume that empty space has no physical qualities whatever. The fundamental facts of mechanics do not harmonize with this view. According to the general theory of relativity, space is endowed with physical qualities; in this sense, there exists an ether. Space without ether is unthinkable (Isaacson, 2007)."

Einstein's resurrected ether begins to sound like our spacetime matrix, accept that Einstein did not see how to integrate quantum theory with spacetime and gravity. Neither did any of the other pioneers of quantum mechanics.

Combining a modified version of Newton's particle concepts (in order to bring them in line with subsequent developments in quantum physics) with a modified version of Einstein's spacetime concepts leads us to our concept of the spacetime matrix. Had these two geniuses been able to converse with one another, the development of theophysics might have taken place much earlier.

RESUMING OUR SURVEY OF THE outline of CGH-1, we have seen how the spacetime matrix is developing in time and is proceeding to approach the limits of the reality bubble. We know that all galaxies are traveling outward from the center of the bubble and away from each other. Now we must keep in mind what many cosmologists and astrophysicists believe, which is that the known universe is *finite yet unbounded.* As with most revolutionary ideas in physics in the twentieth century, this concept originated with Einstein. Walter Isaacson states the following in *Einstein: His Life and Universe:* "It was an idea that initially struck him as so wacky that he told his friend Paul Ehrenfest in Leiden, 'It exposes me to the danger of being confined to a madhouse.' He jokingly asked Ehrenfest for assurances, before he came to visit, that there were no such asylums in Leiden. His new idea was published that month in what became another seminal Einstein paper, 'Cosmological Considerations in the General Theory of Relativity.'

On the surface, it did not seem to be based on a crazy notion: space has no borders because gravity bends it back on itself.

Einstein began by noting that an absolutely infinite universe filled with stars and other objects was not plausible. There would be an infinite amount of gravity tugging at every point and an infinite amount of light shining from every direction. On the other hand, a finite universe floating at some random location in space was not conceivable either. Among other things, what would keep the stars and energy from flying off, escaping, and depleting the universe?

So he developed a third option: a finite universe, but one without boundaries. The masses in the universe caused space to curve, and over the expanse of the universe they caused space (indeed, the whole fourth-dimensional fabric of spacetime) to curve completely in on itself. The system is closed and finite, but there is no end or edge to it (Isaacson, 2007)."

In terms of CGH-1, the spacetime matrix is the entity that curves naturally in on itself as it reaches the boundary of the bubble that the Transcendent Godhead has opened within himself. Thus, although the matrix is finite and unbounded, it reaches a natural limit defined by the gravitational mass of the whole, and this limit corresponds to the limit of the reality bubble.

Once the leading edge of the galaxies and all other matter/energy which comprises the spacetime matrix has reached the limits of the reality bubble, the matrix begins to curve in on itself. The process now reverses. The galaxies are now growing inexorably closer as the matter/energy of the universe heads back to the center of the reality bubble. It is difficult to imagine the catastrophic consequences of this. Yet this is the nature of our universe. It is incomprehensible to our finite minds.

It is clearly impossible for any finite mind to comprehend the infinite mind of God. To put this in the terminology of CGH, it is not possible for a focal manifestation of the Universal Consciousness (Immanent Godhead) to understand the UC, let alone the Transcendent Godhead. We, as FMs, may temporarily merge with the UC through meditation and bring back fragments of what we have experienced, but these fragments can never encompass the whole. This contact is comforting in that we can perceive that the universe is meaningful and that our place in it is important. And formal meditation in the sense that it is practiced in the East is not necessary in order to derive this benefit. Many Christians and Jews, for instance, reap this comfort and understanding through prayer. I mention these two groups because I have experience with members of these groups, but I'm certain that traditional Native American groups, Muslims, and many others also derive spiritual sustenance through contemplative prayer. There is a reason for this. It becomes clear through prayer and meditation that a Creator *actually exists.* Billions of people cannot be deluded. The delusion rests with those who cannot or will not immerse themselves in spiritual practice.

To return to our outline of CGH-1, we have come to the point in our description where the galaxies are returning to the center of the reality bubble. Inexorably, they will all collide and the gravity involved will crush all the matter/ energy into a very small point. Most physicists who believe in universal cycles of expansion and collapse call this point a singularity. We have now returned to the beginning.

Once the universe has collapsed into the singularity, the cycle begins anew. An incredible number of experiences have been accessed by the Transcendent Godhead through the lives of the focal manifestations which, as a totality, constitute the Immanent Godhead.

Now, the universe begins again, possibly with a different set of parameters within which life can exist, possibly not. What is relevant is that the Big Bang recurs, matter and energy again explode out into the reality bubble, life forms again, and an entirely new set of FMs develop and begin to accumulate experiences for the Universal Consciousness.

What makes this a free will scenario is that the physical universe, the spacetime matrix, can be molded by the beliefs of individual conscious entities and groups of entities, and that it is therefore changing and evolving over time. This process was set up by the Transcendent Godhead in order to allow freedom of choice on the part of focal manifestations. The Transcendent Godhead, as part of the set-up of CGH-1, has decided not to view spacetime *en bloc* and thereby allows for free will. Our decisions, choices and beliefs are of paramount importance. They lead to actual changes in the reality around us through their impact on the quantum flux. This is one of the radical implications of quantum mechanics that the majority of physicists shy away from. Only the revolutionaries dare to follow these thoughts through to their logical conclusions. We will consider these thoughts in more detail later, with quotes from scientific pioneers who have pursued them.

WE WILL NOW EXPLORE AN outline of CGH-2. This is the *deterministic scenario* of the Cyclic God Hypothesis. In this scenario, after opening the space within himself, God creates a static spacetime continuum within the entire simple space he's opened within himself and bonds the quantum flux to it. The spacetime matrix is completed in total before consciousness is infused into it.

This may not be immediately comprehensible. To provide clarity, we'll need to investigate what Einstein meant by the term spacetime continuum. Put simply, it unites the three dimensions of space with the dimension of time. We are familiar with all four of these dimensions from everyday experience. A physical object is said to inhabit the three dimensions of space, since it has length, breadth and height. All physical objects, however, also inhabit the dimension of time. Since it is not possible to move in space without moving in time (and vice-versa), the object is said to exist in a four-dimensional spacetime continuum. As we've discussed, the spacetime matrix is a fusion of the spacetime continuum with the quantum or energic flux. But in CGH-2, everything is static. All space, time, matter and energy are forever (or for the life of the universe) frozen in place.

In reference to this topic, Capra quotes physicist Louis DeBroglie as follows: "In spacetime, everything which for us constitutes the past, present, and the future is given *en bloc*... Each observer, as his time passes, discovers, so to speak, new slices of spacetime which appear to him as successive aspects of the material world, though in reality the ensemble of events constituting spacetime exist prior to his knowledge of them (1999)."

So where does movement and life come from? They are brought into existence by the flow of consciousness through the static matrix. As consciousness touches each spacetime coordinate, that coordinate comes to life. The universe appears to develop in time solely because of the passage of the Immanent Godhead through the matrix. But everything has been determined in advance by the Transcendent Godhead. Nothing is left to chance or choice. Free will is absent.

CGH-2 may seem like a nightmare scenario to anyone who considers free will sacrosanct, but from the perspective of each living, conscious being, no sacrilege will have taken place. The world would appear to be inhabited by sentient beings who can freely decide their own fate. Only the Transcendent Godhead would be aware that all was determined beforehand, down to the positions of every last subatomic particle. The illusion would be complete.

So how do we decide which universe we're living in? The answer is, *we don't.* It will never be possible to determine whether we have free will or if our lives and the development of our universe are completely determined. If we make the choice to believe that we're free, that choice may have been built into the matrix from the beginning of time.

My personal choice of scenarios is CGH-1. I choose the free will scenario because I am more comfortable with the thought that my beliefs, decisions and behaviors are freely chosen. It is entirely possible that God alternates scenarios. And in the end, it doesn't matter. If the individual focal manifestations believe they are free, then that perception becomes their reality. We know from experience, of course, that different people believe a wide variety of things about any given topic. I know people who believe that everything is determined and others who strongly believe that they are free. These beliefs are highly relevant if we live in the CGH-1 universe. We will explore belief dynamics in detail in the next chapter.

Before we conclude this chapter, I should mention that anomalous events may occur in both CGH-1 and CGH-2. By this I mean events which appear out of place given the "laws" we have assigned to the world around us. This would include that category of events we commonly call "miracles," as well as inexplicable events noted only by scientists.

In CGH-1, anomalous events occur as a result of the fact that *there are no laws of the universe except that it is malleable with respect to its structure within the parameters of the spacetime matrix.* The quantum flux can produce many different regularities which we take to be laws, but which are actually a result of consensus beliefs among a given group of individuals. This is why reality feels different within different cultures. We call the recognition of this *culture shock.* It is also why the content of our scientific beliefs change over time and why *the "facts" or observations of science change as well.* This is especially true during scientific revolutions, which occur when a sufficiently large number of anomalies begin to make it obvious that the traditional wisdom of science has failed to explain the so-called facts of empirical observation. Reality has undergone a metamorphosis and we haven't caught up.

In CGH-2, anomalies are built into the matrix by the Transcendent Godhead. Strange or miraculous events occur because the Trancendent Godhead anticipates that they will be interesting when experienced by the focal manifestations of the Immanent Godhead. This might include events such as the birth, life, death and resurrection of Messiah Yeshua (the name of Jesus in his native language, Aramaic). Everything to do with that event, according to CGH-2, was pre-programmed into the matrix. In CGH-1, however, it developed in accordance with the beliefs of Yeshua and his followers, and his connections to the Transcendent Godhead, which he called Abba (Papa) or Father. I choose to believe, as I've said, in CGH-1.

4 – BELIEF DYNAMICS

WEBSTER'S DICTIONARY DEFINES *BELIEF* AS "the conviction that certain things are true." *Dynamics* is defined as "the science dealing with motions produced by given forces." I define *belief dynamics* as the study of the impact of beliefs on the forms and movements of the quantum flux. This applies only in CGH-1, wherein the matrix is a medium which is responsive to the beliefs of individuals and groups.

In his book *The Dancing Wu Li Masters,* Gary Zukav states the following: "*The general theory of relativity shows us that our minds follow different rules than the real world does.* A rational mind, based on the impressions that it receives from its limited perspective, forms structures which thereafter determine what it further will or will not accept freely. From that point on, regardless of how the real world actually operates, this rational mind, following its self-imposed rules, tries to superimpose on the real world its own version of what must be (Zukav, 2001)." I would take this one step farther and state that *there is no real world in the sense that science or common sense intends.* The world or universe is comprised of two things only, the matrix and consciousness. We are not simply imposing structure which does not actually exist in the "real world." *Our imposition of structure shapes reality.* In CGH-1, the divided consciousness of the Immanent Godhead is the potter, the spacetime matrix is the clay.

Zukav (2001), speaking about the process of constructing models of reality in physics, states the following: "In 1927, the most famous assemblage of physicists in history decided that it might not ever be possible to construct a model of reality, i.e., to explain the way things 'really are behind the scenes.' Despite the tidal wave of 'knowledge' which has swept over us for forty years, the Fundamental Physics Group (at Lawrence Berkeley Laboratory) found it necessary, like the physicists at Copenhagen a half century before them, to acknowledge that it might not be possible to construct a model of reality. The acknowledgement is more than a recognition of the limitations of this theory or that theory. It is a recognition emerging throughout the West that *knowledge itself* is limited."

This state of affairs is a result of the fact that quantum mechanics can only predict the *probability* that any given event will happen. At the quantum level, particle behavior appears chaotic, with subatomic bundles of energy changing from one form to another and winking in and out of existence. This subatomic level of reality is what I refer to as the quantum flux. This is the level of reality that is impacted by human beliefs and intentions. To achieve this impact, however, it appears necessary to have not only a conscious or unconscious belief or intention, but this belief or intention must be driven by emotion. Referring back to Braden's (2007) statements about the Divine Matrix, we can amend his contention about influencing the matrix through the language of emotion to state that we mold or shape the matrix through *emotively driven beliefs*. Non-directed emotion alone is of little use.

Before we investigate more of the specifics of *belief dynamics*, we will pursue a bit more information about the workings of the quantum world. In his book, *The Tao of Physics* (1999), Dr. Capra states: "The search for the ultimate stuff of the universe ends with the discovery that there *isn't any.*

If there is any ultimate stuff of the universe, it is pure energy, but subatomic particles are not 'made of' energy, they *are* energy. This is what Einstein theorized in 1905. Subatomic interactions, therefore, are interactions of energy with energy. At the subatomic level there is no longer a clear distinction between what is and what happens, between the actor and the action. At the subatomic level the dancer and the dance are one.

According to particle physics, the world is fundamentally dancing energy; energy that is everywhere and incessantly assuming first this form and then that. What we have been calling matter (particles) constantly is being created, annihilated and created again. This happens as particles interact and it also happens, literally, out of nowhere.

Where there was 'nothing,' there suddenly was 'something,' and then the something is gone again, often changing into something else before vanishing. In particle physics there is no distinction between empty, as in 'empty space,' and not-empty, or between something and not-something. The world of particle physics is a world of sparkling energy forever dancing with itself in the form of its particles as they twinkle in and out of existence, collide, transmute and disappear again.

The world view of particle physics is a picture of *chaos beneath order.* At the fundamental level is a confusion of continual creation, annihilation and transformation."

Now we'll return to our discussion of belief dynamics.

Most emotion is generated by thoughts. In fact, very little emotion occurs without being directly generated by preceeding thoughts. These thoughts are often not fully conscious and are sometimes definitively *unconscious*, thus giving the impression that the emotion in question occurred for no particular reason. Generally, however, the relevant thoughts can be retrieved with little difficulty. They are then said to have been in a preconscious or descriptively unconscious state (Freud, 1900). There are thoughts that generate emotion which are *very unavailable* to conscious recall, and these thoughts are said to be dynamically unconscious (Freud, 1900). "Studies of the impact of intention on physical processes show that these results can occur regardless of the level of consciousness of the intention, though unconscious intention is perhaps the most powerful (McTaggart, 2002)."

Thoughts tend to cluster in complexes. These complexes represent beliefs about a given topic. Individual human beings in cultural groups tend to share complexes. These mutually reinforcing belief systems can become very powerful and tend to shape reality, through molding the matrix, in characteristic ways for that culture or group.

Lynne McTaggart, in her book *The Field* (2002), had this to say about the relationship between consciousness and the physical world: "If consciousness itself created order – or indeed in some way created the world – this suggested much more capacity in the human being than we currently understood. It also suggested some revolutionary notions about humans in relation to their world and the relation between all living things... Did living consciousness possess some quantum-field-like properties, enabling it to extend its influence out into the world? If so, was it possible to do more than simply observe? How strong was our influence? It was only a small step in logic to conclude that in our action as an observer in the quantum world, we might also be an influencer, a creator." In a related quote regarding the measurement of human intention on the functioning of machines , McTaggart makes the following statements:

"It appeared that the unconscious mind somehow had the capability of communicating with the sub-tangible physical world – the quantum world of all possibility. This marriage of unformed mind and matter would then assemble itself into something tangible in the manifest world (2002)."

We will shortly consider ways in which we can think about our belief systems which will clarify the power of thoughts, beliefs and intentions, but before we do, we will consider one final quote from *The Field*. In summing up the discoveries of the physicists, biologists and neuroscientists whose work she discusses in her book, McTaggart (2002) states the following: "These scientists had come to the position that the communication of the world did not occur in the visible realm of Newton, but in the subatomic world of Werner Heisenberg. Cells and DNA communicated through frequencies. The brain perceived and made a record of the world in pulsating waves. A substructure underpins the universe that is essentially a recording medium for everything to communicate with everything else. People are indivisible from their environment. Living consciousness is not an isolated entity. It increases order in the rest of the world.

The consciousness of human beings has incredible powers, to heal ourselves, to heal the world – in a sense, to make it as we wish it to be."

I would only add that human beings have these powers because they are *focal manifestations* of the Immanent Godhead.

We'll now consider some ideas derived from the work of Dr. John C. Lilly, a neuroscientist, psychoanalyst and consciousness researcher. The works from which I'll be quoting are *The Center of the Cyclone* (1972) and *The Steersman* (1975).

We'll start be addressing Lilly's distinction between beliefs and metabeliefs. A belief, as we've previously discussed, is a conviction of the truth of something; a collection of thoughts on a particular subject. A metabelief is a *belief about beliefs*. There are many possible beliefs about beliefs, as simple reflection will show. Lilly's contention, however, was that one particular metabelief was primary. He called it the *metabelief operator*. The metabelief operator states that "what one believes to be true is true or becomes true within limits to be found experientially and experimentally. These limits are further beliefs to be transcended. In the province of the mind, there are no limits (1975)."

Human minds have no limits because we have access at times to the Transcendent Godhead. We also have direct access, in some instances, to other focalized minds within the Immanent Godhead. This is accomplished by a process we typically call mental telepathy. This process is also termed *morphic resonance* by the innovative biologist Rupert Sheldrake.

The physical universe presents limits in the form of the spacetime matrix, but can be molded over time within the parameters established by the spacetime continuum and the quantum or energic flux.

I would add to this that the external "realities" can be modified over the short term in such a way that scientific experiments will "confirm" what we believe to be true. This is especially the case when there are no current beliefs about a particular process being studied, or when there are multiple competing beliefs about that process. It is also the case that experimental results can *disconfirm* what we do *not* believe to be true. Physicist Lee Smolin, in his book *The Trouble with Physics* (2006), states the following: "It is often the case that surprising experimental results are not confirmed when other experimentalists repeat the experiment. This does not mean someone is being dishonest. Experiments on the edge of what is possible are almost always hard to replicate." Smolin does not speculate as to why this would be the case, but I would submit that it occurs for the reasons stated above.

In his book *The Steersman,* during a discussion of the nature of objective and subjective reality, Dr. Lilly quotes theologian and philosopher Bishop Berkeley as follows: "All those bodies which compose the mighty frame of the world have not any substance without the mind. So long as they are not perceived by me, or do not exist in my mind, or that of any other created spirit, they must either *have no existence at all, or subsist in the mind of some Eternal Spirit* (1975)."

Both Dr. Lilly and Bishop Berkeley agree that the human mind is a powerful thing, but they *seem* to disagree as to whether or not anything exists outside our minds. Lilly does appear to believe that the mind and the outside physical universe are somehow separate. Numerous caveats appear in Lilly's writings to the effect that there are definite limits imposed by external reality. One such warning appears in the following statement: "Independent realities exist, which do not depend on our belief systems. We project simulations onto these realities, thus confusing what we wish the universe to be with what it is (Lilly, 1975)." Bishop Berkeley is actually in agreement with Lilly, as a careful review of his statement indicates. The "bodies" which Berkeley refers to can exist in the mind of an "Eternal Spirit," as opposed to a "created spirit." Lilly, elsewhere in both *The Center of the Cyclone* and *The Steersman,* does make reference to "the creators," which he appears to believe are independent entities.

What we can take from Lilly and Berkeley is that reality is a fluid thing and that our minds are intimately connected to that fluidity. In fact, our beliefs about reality are an essential ingredient in the mix. In terms of *belief dynamics,* we can say that the contents of our minds, our thoughts, beliefs and emotions taken together, interact in some way with the content of the "external" world.

So how does this take place? How do our emotively driven beliefs impact or interact with the seemingly separate physical processes of the outside world? Before we begin to investigate this topic, I would remind the reader that our contentions apply only to CGH-1, since CGH-2 requires no interaction. Consciousness flows through a static spacetime matrix, activating discrete spacetime coordinates as it proceeds. The matrix does not evolve. All is determined beforehand. Thus, all of our discussions regarding belief dynamics, and indeed much of the discussion in subsequent chapters, apply only to CGH-1. When this is not the case, I'll alert the reader to that fact.

Belief dynamics presupposes *quantum entanglement.* Put simply, quantum entanglement means that any two particles, once in contact, maintain an instantaneous connection with one another no matter what the subsequent distance is between them. This has been demonstrated numerous times experimentally. Information is somehow exchanged between the particles and results in actual changes in behavior of the particles. Physicists do not know how or why this takes place. But the fact remains that it does. Einstein predicted this in one of his famous "thought experiments" (in conjunction with two colleagues, Podolsky and Rosen), but didn't believe it could happen. He called it "spooky action at a distance (Isaacson, 2007)." It is now called *the EPR (Einstein, Podolsky, Rosen) effect.*

What does this have to do with belief dynamics? The connection becomes obvious when we remember three things. The first is that all the matter/energy of the universe was originally in contact in the singularity which existed prior to the Big Bang. The second is that consciousness is attached to all particles. The third is that many conscious entities, during the course of the development of the universe in CGH-1, became *self-conscious.* Putting these three pieces of information together, we can extrapolate that *self-conscious beings can influence the physical universe through some yet-to-be-discovered means.* It has been shown definitively over the past three decades that humans can influence a variety of physical processes through *intention.* McTaggart, in her book *The Field* (2002), investigates the relevant experiments, as previously discussed. Other authors have also investigated these developments.

We will close our investigation of Lilly's contributions to belief dynamics with two quotes. "Basic beliefs are postulates operative through the long term behavior, writings and vocalizations of a given individual. *Belief systems are those vital guides by which we steer our lives.* They are rarely conscious constructions. As with an iceberg, the greater part of our guiding beliefs is below ordinary levels of perception (1975)."

We steer through life by means of our conscious/ unconscious beliefs and belief systems, molding reality as we go, both as individuals and as groups. We can do so more effectively through the use of Lilly's metabelief operator. "What one believes to be true, is true or becomes true within limits to be found through experience and experiment. These limits are further beliefs to be transcended. In the province of the mind, there are no limits (1972)."

Though the extent of impact of the beliefs of any given individual is relatively small, many investigators believe that the compounded intent of many individuals is cumulative. Some experimental evidence for this exists. I have no doubt that large groups of self-conscious beings over extended periods of time *do* in fact influence and shape physical reality.

We'll continue our investigation of belief dynamics by considering some of the work of Carlos Castaneda, a brilliant and controversial anthropologist who apprenticed himself to the Yaqui Indian shaman don Juan Matus during the 1960s. We will start our discussion with an extended quote from Castaneda's commentary introducing the 30 year anniversary edition of his first book, *The Teachings of Don Juan: A Yaqui Way of Knowledge* (1998), as follows: "The irreducible description of what I did in the field would be to say that the Yaqui Indian sorcerer, don Juan Matus, introduced me into the *cognition* of the shamans of ancient Mexico. By *cognition* is meant the processes responsible for the awareness of everyday life, processes which include memory, experience, perception, and the expert use of a given syntax.

For the sorcerers of don Juan's lineage… there is the *cognition* of modern man, and there is the *cognition* of the shamans of ancient Mexico. Don Juan considered these to be entire worlds of everyday life which were intrinsically different from one another. At a given moment, unbeknownst to me, my task mysteriously shifted from the mere gathering of anthropological data to the internalization of the new cognitive processes of the shaman's world…

Little did I know at that time that don Juan was not giving me just an appealing intellectual description; he was describing something he called an *energetic fact*. *Energetic facts,* for him, were the conclusions that he and other shamans of his lineage arrived at when they engaged in a function which they called *seeing*: the act of perceiving energy directly as it flows in the universe. The capacity to perceive energy in this manner is one of the culminating points of shamanism...

Don Juan said that the *energetic fact* which was the cornerstone of the *cognition* of the shamans of ancient Mexico was that every nuance of the cosmos is an expression of energy...

To perceive energy directly allowed the sorcerers of don Juan's lineage to *see* human beings as conglomerates of energy fields that have the appearance of luminous balls. Observing human beings in such a fashion allowed these shamans to draw extraordinary energetic conclusions. They noticed that each of the luminous balls is individually connected to an energetic mass of inconceivable proportions which they called *the dark sea of awareness.* They observed that each individual ball is attached to the *dark sea of awareness* at a point that is even more brilliant than the luminous ball itself. Those shamans called that point of juncture *the assemblage point,* because they observed that it is at that spot that perception takes place. The flux of energy at large is turned, at that point, into sensorial data, and those data are then interpreted as the world that surrounds us...

What the shamans of ancient Mexico found out when they focused their *seeing* on the *dark sea of awareness* was the revelation that the entire cosmos is made of luminous filaments that extend themselves infinitely. Shamans describe them as luminous filaments that go every which way without ever touching one another. They *saw* that they are individual filaments, and yet they are grouped in inconceivably enormous masses.

Another of such masses of filaments, besides *the dark sea of awareness* which the shamans observed and liked because of its vibration, was something they called *intent,* and the act of individual shamans focusing their attention on such a mass, was something they called *intending.* They *saw* that the entire universe was a universe of *intent,* and *intent,* for them, was the equivalent of intelligence. Their conclusion, which became part of their *cognitive world,* was that vibratory energy, aware of itself, was intelligent in the extreme. They saw that the mass of *intent* in the cosmos was responsible for all the possible mutations, all the possible variations which happened in the universe, not because of arbitrary, blind circumstances, but because of the *intending* done by the vibratory energy, at the level of the flux of energy itself...

The *energetic fact* of the universe being composed of luminous filaments gave rise to the shamans' conclusion that each of those filaments that extend themselves infinitely is a field of energy. They observed that luminous filaments, or rather fields of energy of such a nature converge on and go through the *assemblage point.* Since the size of the *assemblage point* was determined to be equivalent to that a modern tennis ball, only a finite number of energy fields... converge on and go through that spot.

When the sorcerers of ancient Mexico *saw* the *assemblage point,* they discovered the *energetic fact* that the impact of the energy fields going through the *assemblage point* was transformed into sensory data; data which were then interpreted into the *cognition* of the world of everyday life." (Italics in original)

We have in Castaneda's description of the Toltec shamans' world many of the ingredients of the Cyclic God Hypothesis. We have temporal-spatial energy fields with consciousness, points of connection between human beings and these energy fields, and the assembling of reality constructs through the interaction of humans with the energic flux through intent. Finally, from elsewhere in Castaneda's writings, we have the construction of different sensory/perceptual consensus realities as a result of different positions of the assemblage point on the luminous egg or ball of the human being. This corresponds to our description of the construction of different realities among different cultural groups or subgroups.

It should be noted that these cultural groups and subgroups need not be ethnic. One non-ethnic cultural group is that of scientists in general, and one subgroup of scientists is composed of physicists. Each group and subgroup has its own consensus reality and its own special language to both convey and to shape that reality.

It is my belief that some of the problems in contemporary physics in reaching consensus on an overarching theory occur as a result of the fact that more physicists are alive and working today than in all the years of the history of science combined. This leads to the need to incorporate ever growing numbers of ideas and conflicting experimental observations into the models being developed to understand the physical universe. According to physicist and author Lee Smolin, very little progress has been made in the past three decades. The most popular current candidate for a "theory of everything" is Superstring Theory, but there are serious problems associated with the theory. Readers interested in a treatment of those issues from the pen of an expert should consult Smolin's book *The Trouble with Physics* (2006).

It should also be noted that the *"theory of everything"* currently being pursued by physicists is not actually worthy of the name, since it leaves out both consciousness and God. Any theory of everything that leaves out the most important things is actually just a theory of the *material* universe. I would encourage any physicists among my readership to look past my layman's presentation and see the core concepts as critically important to our understanding of our physical world, our*selves* and our Creator. *Theophysics,* properly developed, is the wave of the future.

Belief dynamics is also operative in the healing arts. The field of energy healing has numerous practitioners who explain the basis of their work in different ways. *Matrix Energetics* is one example (Bartlett, 2007). All can be subsumed under belief dynamics.

In closing our chapter on belief dynamics, we can note that *beliefs interact with the "material world" through the quantum flux.* Consensus realities are built through commonly held group beliefs. Group beliefs shape the world perceived by that group. All groups taken together shape the consensus reality of humanity.

5 – Miracles, Mysticism
And The Matrix

Nature, as conceptualized by average physicists, is often viewed (perhaps unconsciously) as separate from the humans who observe it. My contention is that physicists sometimes find the truth of the underlying reality (which includes us) and at other times find only the phantasms of the quantum flux. Mystics often find underlying reality, only to be unable to express their findings in a way which seems relevant to everyday life. But the findings of each, conveyed properly, can change our experience of the world.

Physicists discovered a critical reality when they developed field theories. Spacetime is a field. Quantum theory presented what initially looked like an insoluble problem for field theories, in that quanta were discrete units of matter and energy. This was overcome with the advent of quantum field theories. In CGH 1 and 2, the separation between the spacetime continuum and the quantum flux is overcome in the concept of the spacetime matrix. Both are simply aspects of one entity, and this one entity, the matrix, gives rise to the physical aspects of the focal manifestations (FMs) of the Immanent Godhead.

Capra expressed the matter as follows: "In quantum field theories, the classical contrast between the solid particles and the space surrounding them is completely overcome. The quantum field is seen as the fundamental physical entity; a continuous medium which is present everywhere in space. Particles are merely local condensations of the field; concentrations of energy which come and go, thereby losing their individual character and dissolving into the underlying field. In the words of Albert Einstein: 'We may therefore regard matter as being constituted by the regions of space in which the field is extremely intense… There is no place in this new kind of physics both for the field and matter, for the field is the only reality (1999).'"

Capra continues: "The conception of physical things and phenomena as transient manifestations of an underlying fundamental entity is not only a basic element of quantum field theory, but also a basic element of the Eastern world view. Like Einstein, the Eastern mystics consider this underlying entity as the only reality: all its phenomenal manifestations are seen as transitory and illusory. The intuition behind the physicist's interpretation of the subatomic world, in terms of the quantum field, is closely paralleled by the Eastern mystic, who interprets his or her experience of the world in terms of an ultimate underlying reality. Subsequent to the emergence of the field concept, physicists have attempted to unify the various fields into a single fundamental field which would incorporate all physical phenomena. Einstein, in particular, spent the last years of his life searching for such a unified field theory. The Brahman of the Hindus, like the Dharmakaya of the Buddhists and the Tao of the Taoists, can be seen, perhaps, as the ultimate unified field from which spring not only the phenomena studied in physics, but all other phenomena as well (1999)."

The Cyclic God Hypothesis *is* a unified field theory which incorporates within its metabelief structure *all* of the complementary beliefs of *all* mysticism (both Eastern and Western) and Western science.

I'd like to point out at this point that *Western* mysticism also incorporates a concept of the unity of all finite beings within a transcendent being. This is prominently the case in the writings of the two great mystics of early Christianity, the apostles Paul and John of the New Testament. Paul repeatedly talks about Christians being part of the Body of Christ, and John states that Christ created all things and is a part of all things. Paul states that it is within Christ that we "live and move and have our being (Acts 17:28)." Christ is seen as an aspect of the Transcendent Godhead *and* as a focal manifestation of the Immanent Godhead with respect to his corporeal existence as Jesus of Nazareth two millennia ago.

Whereas Capra focused on the similarities between *Eastern* mysticism and quantum mechanics, I will focus on the parallels between *Western* mysticism and aspects of the Cyclic God Hypothesis. Specifically, I'll be examining mystical elements in the practices of Messiah Jesus and his apostles, along with those same elements in the practice of Old Testament prophets. Since belief dynamics is the key to both CGH and mysticism, we will examine the connection between the two.

Why mysticism in particular? This is perhaps a good time to remind the reader of my belief that focal manifestations (including you and I) need to be periodically reconnected to the Transcendent Godhead in order to remember who we are, or at least that God exists. Mysticism provides a direct connection to the Source. It is an *experience* of God, rather than simply an intellectual *faith in* or *assent to* the existence of God. The difference is important.

In examining the New Testament, we must not overlook the man about whom Paul, John, and the rest of the apostles were speaking. That is, of course, Jesus of Nazareth. Jesus was said to be the Messiah, which simply means "anointed one." He was thought to be anointed by God for the work of bringing mankind back to a close relationship with God. And Jesus said on many occasions that "I and the Father are one (John 10:30)," or that "The Father is in me, and I in Him (John 10:38)." I am not the only person who has read these words and heard in them the proclamations of a mystic. So we shall also be investigating the words and deeds of Messiah

Jesus. In the statements quoted above, Jesus is clearly saying that he, as a human being (focal manifestation), is a part of God the Father (the Transcendent Godhead). These are undeniably the words of a mystic and are clear indicators that mysticism is an important part of human existence *and Christianity,* which has been recalled by some.

From a CGH perspective (1 *or* 2), Yeshua is claiming that he is fully conscious of being part of the Transcendent Godhead, but it is clear that he wanted *all* of his followers to attain to this same awareness regarding themselves. He did *not* claim to be the only son of the Father, as has been mistakenly believed to be the case, but believed and *stated* that we are *all* sons and daughters of God. We will shortly consider some quotes from the Bible in support of my claim. There is also supporting documentation in some of the Gnostic texts which were discovered near Nag Hammadi, Egypt, in 1945. Orthodox Christians reject these documents, however, and I therefore consider it important to support my claims directly from the Bible wherever possible. I ask my Christian readers to remain as open-minded as possible, and I ask this of my non-Christian readers as well. Those interested in the Gnostic texts should consult the text of the *Nag Hammadi Library* (Robinson, 1990).

It is also true that mystics of the Old and New Testament periods were healers. The type of healing they typically engaged in is now commonly called *faith healing.* It is clearly a practice involving *belief dynamics.* In the New Testament, Jesus was a belief healer without peer, though it is true that both during his ministry and after his death, his closest disciples also healed many. In the following paragraphs we'll consider some of Yeshua's healings and what he had to say about them. All selections will come from the New King James Version of the Bible.

In Matthew, chapter 7, verses 5-10 and 13, we find the following: "Now when Jesus had entered Capernaum, a centurion came to Him, saying, 'Lord, my servant is lying at home paralyzed, dreadfully tormented.'

And Jesus said to him, 'I will come and heal him.'

The centurion answered and said, 'Lord, I am not worthy that You should come under my roof. But only speak a word, and my servant will be healed. For I, also, am a man under authority, having soldiers under me. I say to this one, 'Go,' and he goes; and to another, 'Come,' and he comes; and to my servant, 'Do this,' and he does it.'

When Jesus heard it, He marveled, and said to those who followed, 'Assuredly, I say to you, I have not found such great faith, not even in Israel!'

Then Jesus said to the centurion, 'Go your way; and *as you have believed*, so let it be done to you.' And his servant was healed that same hour." (Italics mine)

There are three important points to note regarding this healing, and all are intimately tied to theophysics and belief dynamics. First, the belief involved was *not* that of the "patient," but of the advocate for the patient. Second, the healing was done *at a distance*. And third, it took place *instantaneously*. There is clearly much more at work here than simple faith healing. The matrix is being consciously impacted by an experienced practitioner of *quantum belief engineering* (my term), the practical application of belief dynamics.

For another example, we go to Matthew, chapter 17, verses 14-21, and find the following: "And when they came to the multitude, a man came to Him, kneeling down to Him and saying, 'Lord, have mercy on my son, for he is an epileptic and suffers severely; for he often falls into the fire and often into the water. So I brought him to your disciples, but they could not cure him.'

Then Jesus answered and said, 'O faithless and perverse generation, how long shall I be with you? Bring him here to Me.' And Jesus rebuked the demon, and it came out of him; and the child was cured from that very hour.

Then the disciples came to Jesus privately, and said, 'Why could we not cast it out?'

So Jesus said to them, *'Because of your unbelief*; for assuredly, I say to you, if you have faith as a mustard seed, you will say to this mountain, 'Move from here to there,' and it will move; and nothing will be impossible for you. However, this kind comes out only through prayer and fasting." (Italics mine)

Two points are clear in this passage; that powerful belief can accomplish what many of us would call miracles, and that deep focus in the form of "prayer and fasting," also known as meditation, may be necessary to eradicate longstanding, difficult conditions.

Webster's Dictionary defines a miracle as, "an event or action which appears to contradict known scientific laws." Scientific "laws," however, are in the process of being overhauled. What we have believed to be true of the physical universe is, in many cases, no longer accepted as true. The 20th century saw an incredible revolution in our views of "scientific truth," and the reverberations of that revolution are still being felt.

It is my contention, of course, that the only "law" in existence with regard to the physical universe is that which governs the functioning of the spacetime matrix. The law, in essence, is that our individual and communal beliefs help to shape the world which we apprehend through our senses.

Another example of belief engineering in action appears in Matthew, chapter 21, verses 18-22, where we are told the following: "Now in the morning, as He returned to the city, He was hungry. And seeing a fig tree by the road, He came to it and found nothing on it but leaves, and said to it, 'Let no fruit grow on you ever again.' Immediately the fig tree withered away.

And when the disciples saw it, they marveled, saying, 'How did the fig tree wither away so soon?'

So Jesus answered and said to them, 'Assuredly, I say to you, if you have faith *and do not doubt*, you will not only do what was done to the fig tree, but also if you say to this mountain, 'Be removed and be cast into the sea,' it will be done. And whatever things you ask in prayer, *believing*, you will receive." (Italics mine)

What we immediately notice in this example is that *there was no believing recipient of this action*. The belief resided entirely within Jesus himself. And Jesus asserts that his disciples will be able to accomplish the same and even greater feats of belief engineering *if they believe without doubt*.

We'll consider two more examples from Yeshua's ministry and then proceed to other individuals.

In the gospel of Mark, chapter 5, verses 25-34, we're told the following: "Now a certain woman had a flow of blood for twelve years, and had suffered many things from many physicians. She had spent all that she had and was no better, but rather grew worse. When she heard about Jesus, she came behind Him in the crowd and touched his garment. For she said, 'If only I may touch His clothes, I shall be made well.'

Immediately, the fountain of her blood was dried up, and she felt in her body that she was healed of the affliction. And Jesus, immediately knowing in Himself that power had gone out of Him, turned around in the crowd and said, 'Who touched my clothes?'

But his disciples said to Him, 'You see the multitude thronging You, and You say, 'Who touched me?'

And He looked around to see her who had done this thing. But the woman, fearing and trembling, knowing what had happened to her, came and fell down before Him and told Him the whole truth. And he said to her, 'Daughter, your *faith* has made you well. Go in peace, and be healed of your affliction." (Italics mine)

In this example, it is clear that the belief resides in the recipient of the healing. The "healer" himself is not consciously involved.

Our last example of belief engineering in the ministry of Jesus follows immediately after the incident of the woman with an issue of blood. In the gospel of Luke, chapter 8, verses 49-56, we are told the following: "While He was still speaking, someone came from the ruler of the synagogue's house, saying to him, 'Your daughter is dead, do not trouble the Teacher.' But when Jesus heard it, He answered him, saying, 'Do not be afraid; *only believe*, and she will be made well.' When He came into the house, He permitted no one to go in except Peter, James, and John, and the father and mother of the girl.

Now all wept and mourned for her; but He said, 'Do not weep, she is not dead, but sleeping.' And they ridiculed Him, knowing that she was dead.

But He put them all outside, took her by the hand, and called, saying, 'Little girl, arise.' Then her spirit returned, and she arose immediately. And He commanded that she be given something to eat. And her parents were astonished, but He charged them to tell no one what had happened." (Italics mine)

There are many liberal Bible scholars who assert that Jesus could not have raised someone from the dead and that the girl must have had a condition that mimicked death. Such conditions are not unknown in our present day. But Jesus was said to have raised more than one person from the dead, and the probability of his having encountered such a medical condition more than once during a three year (or possibly only one year) ministry is vanishingly small. In addition, some of his disciples were said to have raised the dead, and more than one healer in the Old Testament is credited with the same accomplishment. To believe that all of these people *did not* raise the dead is to believe that numerous people surrounding these healers ignorantly believed someone to be dead when such was not the case. Sometimes *not believing* is the ignorant stance.

In the case above, it appears that only Jesus, or perhaps also the three close disciples who were with him, believed that he could raise this girl. Something phenomenal clearly occurred.

If belief is as critical to the process of interacting with the quantum flux as I contend, then there should be instances in the practice of even someone as powerful as Jesus when belief engineering is unable to accomplish its purpose. And so we will report an instance of failure in Yeshua's ministry before moving on to other individuals.

"Then He went out from there and came to His own country, and His disciples followed Him. And when the Sabbath had come, He began to teach in the synagogue. And many hearing Him were astonished, saying, 'Where did this man get these things? And what wisdom is this which is given to him, that such mighty works are performed by his hands? Is this not the carpenter, the son of Mary, and brother of James, Joses, Judas, and Simon? And are not his sisters with us?' So they were offended at Him.

But Jesus said to them, 'A prophet is not without honor, accept in his own country, and in his own house.'

Now He could do no mighty work there, because of their unbelief (Matthew 13:57-58)." (Italics mine)

This incident points out clearly that strong unbelief on the part of observers or recipients of a belief engineering intervention may result in poor or negative results.

I should point out that if Jesus was a mystic, then he certainly taught this practice to his closest disciples. Bible scholar and religion professor Dr. Bruce Chilton believes that this was, in fact, the case. In his book *Rabbi Jesus*, Chilton makes the case that Jesus was a Chariot mystic (referring to the mystical Chariot which carried the Throne of God, seen in a vision by the prophet Elijah). Readers who are interested in an excellent biography of Jesus should consult Chilton's book.

WE'LL NOW INVESTIGATE HEALING ENCOUNTERS involving some of the well known disciples of Jesus. In the Book of Acts (more fully, The Acts of the Apostles), verses 1-10, we read the following: "Now Peter and John went up together to the temple at the hour of prayer, the ninth hour. And a certain man lame from his mother's womb was carried, whom they laid at the gate of the temple which is called Beautiful, to ask alms from those who entered the temple; who, seeing Peter and John about to go into the temple, asked for alms. And fixing his eyes on him, with John, Peter said, 'Look at us.' So he gave them his attention, expecting to receive something from them. Then Peter said, 'Silver and gold I do not have, but what I do have I give you. In the name of Jesus Christ of Nazareth, *rise up and walk.*' And he took him by the right hand and lifted him up, *and immediately his feet and ankle bones received strength.* So he, leaping up, stood and walked and entered the temple with them – walking, leaping and praising God. And all the people saw him walking and praising God. Then they knew that it was he who sat begging alms at the Beautiful Gate of the temple; and they were filled with wonder and amazement at what had happened to him." (Italics mine)

So it is not only the Master who can perform wondrous feats of healing. Those disciples who had been instructed in mysticism and meditation also became masters of belief engineering. Lest it be thought that my comments concerning meditation and mysticism on the part of Yeshua's disciples is without documentation in the New Testament, I refer the reader to Acts 10: 9-17, wherein Peter is praying on a housetop, falls into a trance and has an extensive vision. This type of deep, prolonged prayer *is* meditation and *is* a mystical practice.

Now we'll consider the case of the apostle Paul. Paul was not a disciple of Jesus during his three year ministry prior to the crucifixion. Paul comes into the picture after Yeshua's death. Paul was a member of the Pharisees, one of the Jewish religious groups which were in opposition to Yeshua's teachings, and the group which figures most prominently in the four gospels. We first encounter Paul (as Saul) in the Book of the Acts of the Apostles, where he is persecuting Christians (who at that time were called followers of the Way). In Acts 9:1-9, we are told the following: "Then Saul, still breathing threats and murder against the disciples of the Lord, went to the High Priest and asked letters of him to the synagogues of Damascus, so that if he found any who were of the Way, he might bring them bound to Jerusalem.

As he journeyed he came near Damascus, and suddenly a light shone around him from heaven. Then he fell to the ground and heard a voice saying to him, 'Saul, Saul, why are you persecuting Me?'

And he said, 'Who are you, Lord?'

Then the Lord said, 'I am Jesus, whom you are persecuting...'

So he, trembling and astonished, said, 'Lord, what do you want me to do?'

And the men who journeyed with him stood speechless, hearing a voice, but seeing no one. Then Saul arose from the ground, and when his eyes were opened he saw no one. But they led him by the hand and brought him into Damascus. And he was three days without sight, and neither ate nor drank."

This experience of Paul's clearly can be described as a vision, and it led to Paul's almost immediate conversion to the Way of Messiah Jesus. It also led to many years of tireless and dangerous ministry on Paul's part which included further mystical experiences. Paul's letters, which constitute the majority of the New Testament works, give ample evidence of a mystical outlook on life. Noted biblical scholar and author Bruce Chilton, mentioned previously in connection with his biography of Jesus, also wrote an excellent biography of the apostle Paul in which he documents his assertion that Paul, like Jesus, was a Chariot mystic. Readers interested in this documentation should consult his book, entitled *Rabbi Paul* (Chilton, 2005).

Let us consider some incidents involving Paul following his conversion.

1. In Acts 14: 8-11, we find the following: "... in Lystra a certain man without strength in his feet was sitting, a cripple from his mother's womb, who had never walked. This man heard Paul speaking. Paul, observing him intently and *seeing he had faith to be healed,* said with a loud voice, 'Stand up straight on your feet!' And he leaped and walked." (Italics mine)

2. In Acts 16: 9-10 (regarding mystical visions), we find the following: "And a vision appeared to Paul in the night. A man of Macedonia stood and pleaded with him, saying, 'Come over to Macedonia and help us.' Now after he had seen the vision, immediately we sought to go to Macedonia, concluding that the Lord had called us to preach the gospel to them."

3. In Acts 20: 7-10,12 (regarding raising the dead), we find the following: "Now on the first day of the week, when the disciples came together to break bread, Paul, ready to depart the next day, spoke to them and continued his message until midnight. There were many lamps in the upper room where they were gathered together. And in a window sat a certain young man named Eutychus, who was sinking into a deep sleep. He was overcome by sleep, and as Paul continued speaking, he fell down from the third story and was taken up dead. But Paul went down, fell on him, and embracing him said, 'Do not trouble yourselves, for his life is in him.' And they brought the young man in alive, and they were not a little comforted."

Having visions, healing the sick (including many who have diseases *which are incurable even today with our advanced medical science*), raising the dead, and impacting the physical environment are practices which are characteristic of mystics. And these practices are by no means restricted to biblical times. They are practiced by mystics in *our* time. All are a result of interactions between the consciousness of the practitioner and the spacetime matrix.

Jesus reportedly turned water into wine (John 2:1-11), calmed a storm and walked on water, in addition to allowing his disciple Peter to walk on water, *until Peter lost his faith (belief) that it was possible* (Matthew 14:28-32).

Other practices documented among mystics of our own day include telepathy, psychokinesis, clairvoyance, psychometry, levitation, and the voluntary control of supposedly involuntary bodily processes. Even non-mystics can be taught to believe that such feats are possible and to perform them. Three obvious examples are remote viewing, walking on burning coals without harming the feet, and controlling blood pressure. Additionally, practitioners of intercessory prayer from a variety of faiths have demonstrated, under controlled conditions, the ability to heal serious illnesses and shorten the period of convalescence.

There are undoubtedly other examples with which I'm not personally familiar. It is my contention that all of these practices involve interactions, conscious or unconscious, between human beings and the spacetime matrix.

We'll now turn to the apostle John. John is credited with the last of the four gospels and three letters. His gospel is the most obviously mystical and he, in addition to Paul, described Jesus of Nazareth not only as an earthly Messiah but as the pre-existent cosmic Christ.

John's gospel begins in a way which still inspires me with awe after many readings. In John 1:1-5, we find the following: "In the beginning was the Word, and the Word was with God, and the Word was God. He was in the beginning with God. All things were made through Him, and without Him nothing was made that was made. In Him was life, and the life was the light of men. And the light shines in the darkness, and the darkness does not comprehend it."

John does not report on his own practice of belief engineering, but he does give us clues to how he was able to maintain his type of faith, which is not simply intellectual assent to particular propositions, but is a mystical form of consciousness. In his first Epistle (letter), John states the following: "This is the message which we have heard from Him and declare to you, that God is light and in Him is no darkness at all. If we say that we have fellowship with Him (the Transcendent Godhead, the Father), we lie and do not practice the truth. But if we walk in the light, as He is in the light, we have fellowship with one another, and the blood of Jesus Christ His Son cleanses us from all sin (1 John 1:5-7)."

And the following: "Now by this we know that we know Him, if we keep His commandments. He who says, 'I know Him,' and does not keep His commandments, is a liar, and the truth is not in him. But whoever keeps His word (God the Son, Yeshua), truly the love of God is perfected in him. By this we know that we are in Him. He who says he abides in Him ought himself to walk just as He walked (1 John 2:3-6)."

And this: "He who says he is in the light, and hates his brother, is in darkness until now. He who loves his brother abides in the light, and there is no cause for stumbling in him. But he who hates his brother is in darkness and walks in darkness, and does not know where he is going, because the darkness has blinded his eyes (1 John 2:9-11)."

And this: "Do not love the world or the things in the world. If anyone loves the world, the love of the Father is not in him. For all that is in the world – the lust of the flesh, the lust of the eyes, and the pride of life – is not of the Father but is of the world. And the world is passing away, and the lust of it; but he who does the will of God abides forever (1 John 2:15-17)."

What John is describing is a way of life which promotes human love and community, and allows for encounters with the Transcendent Godhead. When this occurs, belief engineering becomes possible.

....

WE WILL NOW CONSIDER INFORMATION derived from the Old Testament. First, it's important to realize that the "Old Testament" of the Christian Bible is also the entirety of the Jewish Bible. It contains what religious Jews call *the Torah, the Prophets, and the Writings.* So, two ancient religions are represented in this one volume. The Christian writings are approximately two millennia old, and the Jewish writings go back approximately four millennia.

Most of the prophets mentioned in the Old Testament spoke out to the powerful rulers of their time in order to bring the people back to an observance of God's ways. This aspect of their work may be called *forthtelling*. The prophet spoke what he believed were messages directly from God. Prophets also occasionally practiced *foretelling*, in which predictions for the future were made. In addition to these two functions, the prophet often was also a healer *and* was able to impact the processes of nature. Most had visions. All practiced the intensive form of prayer that I have called a form of meditation. All, in my opinion, were mystics.

We will consider two prophets whose exploits are documented in the first and second book of Kings, Elijah and his disciple Elisha.

Elijah practiced his calling during the time of a wicked king named Ahab, whose equally wicked wife was the infamous Jezebel. Ahab and Jezebel, rather than worshiping the Lord God of Israel, worshiped instead the god Baal of the Canaanites. Elijah was sent to Ahab by God with the following message: "As the Lord God of Israel lives, before whom I stand, there shall not be dew nor rain these years, accept at my word (1 Kings 17:1)." God then told Elijah to go to a place where he would be provided food and water (this was fortunate, since staying anywhere near Ahab would undoubtedly have led to a horrible and ignominious death). This drought then actually took place. So we see Elijah's ability to impact the physical environment, through the power of the Lord of Israel (the Transcendent Godhead).

Elijah then feels led by God to go to the house of a widow living in a town near Sidon. The widow lives with her young son, and both are close to starvation. The widow tells Elijah that she was about to make the last of her flour and oil into a last meal for herself and her son. We are told the following: "And Elijah said to her, 'Do not fear; go and do as you have said, but make me a small cake from it first, and bring it to me; and afterward make some for yourself and your son. For thus says the Lord God of Israel: 'The bin of flour shall not be used up, nor shall the jar of oil run dry, until the day the Lord sends rain on the earth.'

So she went away and did according to the word of Elijah; and she and her household ate for many days. The bin of flour was not used up, nor did the jar of oil run dry, according to the word of the Lord which He spoke by Elijah (I Kings 17:12-16)."

We see in this example that Elijah was able to multiply food, as did Jesus on more than one occasion with bread and fish (Mark 6:35-44). Before we go on, I will point out that it is not necessary to believe that Elijah accomplished these feats because of the God he believes in. It is only necessary to observe that *he* believed this. *The process of belief is more important than the content of belief.* I'd also like to point out that these stories are typically dismissed by the non-religious as beyond belief (for them) and therefore untrue. And again I'll state that many of the "miraculous" feats of the Old Testament prophets and New Testament apostles and disciples are duplicated in our time by *our* mystics. *Some are not,* and I would submit that those accomplishments which are no longer observed *are those for which the greatest degree of unbelief is present in the surrounding culture.*

Elijah, like Jesus, Paul, and others in both the Old and New Testaments, resurrected someone from the dead (I Kings 17:8-24), but this is something which we no longer observe today. It is common to believe that it has never happened at all, then or now, *because it's impossible.* And in our scientific, rational, skeptical culture *we may not allow it to be possible.* We believe in science as others believe in religion. Science, for many of us, *is* our religion. I call it Scientism, and its followers are as closed to evidence which challenges their faith as the most ardent Jews, Christians, Muslims, Hindus, Buddhists, or Wiccans. *There is a core of truth in science, as we've been exploring in this book.* There is also a core of truth in all other faiths. *That core is a metabelief.* It is a belief in the power of belief. Now is the time to face that truth.

"What one believes to be true is true or becomes true within limits to be found through experience and experiment. These limits are further beliefs to be transcended. In the province of the mind, there are no limits (Lilly, 1972)."

I've mentioned previously that different cultures form different consensus realities. The belief parameters of these different consensus realities allow for things to happen in one reality which are not allowed to happen in others. India allows different things than Indiana. China allows different things than Alaska. There is, however, an underlying reality (as Einstein also believed) which is the same *no matter where you are on Earth or in the greater cosmos.* This, to me, is comforting. And, as we've previously seen, that underlying reality is the spacetime matrix, a compound structure comprised of Einstein's spacetime continuum and the quantum flux.

In CGH-1 and CGH-2, consciousness flows through the matrix. The coordinates of the matrix through which mobile consciousness is flowing determines the experiences which are either created freely or endured passively. It behooves us to act *as if* we are free and choosing our realities. If we are, then we can make a decision to leave the spacetime coordinates which contain negative experiences and move on to those which contain positive experiences. The transition may not be immediate, but making the choice begins the process.

We can even choose to begin a journey which brings us to exotic coordinates within the matrix. We could, for example, begin a journey toward a space wherein time travel is possible. Ordinarily, in our current "neighborhood" in the matrix, we *choose* (unconsciously, due to currently operative belief systems) to flow *forward* in time. Travelling backward in time will only become possible when our belief systems have changed sufficiently to embrace this possibility.

We'll now briefly consider the case of Elisha, Elijah's disciple, who became just as powerful as his teacher.

Elisha, like Elijah before him, and like Jesus and *his* disciples *after* him, was able to raise the dead. In 2 Kings 4:30-37, Elisha restores life to the child of a Shunammite woman. 2 Kings 6:11-12 gives evidence of either telepathy or clairaudience (hearing from afar). In 2 Kings 5:9-14, Elisha facilitates the healing of an army commander from leprosy. In 2 Kings 6:16-18, he causes a young associate to have a vision, and shortly afterward strikes the members of an invading army with blindness.

Again, our modern cynicism rebels at the thought of these accomplishments. But these are not fairy tales. They are revered religious writings which have been preserved for posterity with an eye toward accuracy of transmission. And they are clearly *not* meant to be taken as symbolic, but rather as historical documents.

What we *can* say, however, is that *reality was much more fluid* at the time of these writings. And that fluidity was maintained globally until four to five centuries ago, when the new religion of Scientism began to encroach on the cognitive territory which had been shared amicably by numerous belief systems until that time. In Western culture, Scientism has run roughshod over all competing belief systems, *claiming not to be a belief system but only an inventory of the facts of the human world and the greater cosmos.* Fortunately, Scientism is collapsing from within and will eventually have to accept a much more humble position as one belief system among many. Those who choose Scientism will know they are choosing from among a plurality of ways to understand the world. They will choose it for the same reason that others choose Buddhism, Christianity, Shamanism, Astrology or any other belief system. They will do it because it fits their *cognitive style*.

It is important to the Transcendent Godhead that no one belief system should supplant all the rest. It is preferable that as many belief systems as possible should be represented. The reason for this is clear. *You and I are here to have experiences for God.* That is our purpose. *And we are all a part of God by virtue of being focal manifestations of the Immanent Godhead.* That is who we are. We have God within us. *And we came from the Transcendent Godhead.* So the three eternal questions which humans have asked for millennia are now answered.

6 – THEOPSYCHOLOGY AND THEOPHYSICS

THEOPSYCHOLOGY IS THE STUDY OF the mind of God. Theophysics is the study of the physical universe which God has created inside the reality bubble. These two studies are intimately related.

In this short chapter we'll be tying together the various threads of the tapestry we're calling the Cyclic God Hypothesis. CGH can be seen as an updated version of the core of truth in Hindu philosophy (and the Western Perennial Philosophy). This truth concerns the concepts of Brahman and Atman.

Brahman corresponds to the Transcendent Godhead and Atman to the focal manifestations which, taken together, comprise the Immanent Godhead. In Hindu philosophy, specifically in the Upanishads, God is pictured as playing a game of hide-and-seek with himself. He appears as the innumerable actors in the grand play which is the developing universe. Hence, the psychology which we're describing is a religious psychology, as is inevitable, given that *the entire physical universe and that which is outside it consists entirely of God. There is nothing but God.* But we should not confuse the FMs with the UC. *Megalomania is not our goal or our point.* As individual human beings *we are not God.* And all human beings taken together *are not God.* All sentient beings in the universe *are not God.* But all sentient beings in the universe are and always have been God, *once they have awakened to that awareness as one.* That awakening occurs outside of time and space.

The Indian epic, the *Mahabharata,* contains the very popular religious text called the *Bhagavad Gita.* The *Gita* is a dialogue between the god Krishna and the warrior Arjuna. Though set in the background of a battle, the dialogue is actually spiritual instruction. Capra (1999) states the following: "The basis of Krishna's spiritual instruction, as of all Hinduism, is the idea that the multitude of things and events around us are but different manifestations of the same ultimate reality. This reality, called Brahman, is the unifying concept which gives Hinduism its essentially monistic character in spite of the worship of numerous gods and goddesses.

Brahman, the ultimate reality, is understood as the soul, the inner essence, of all things... The manifestation of Brahman in the human soul is called Atman, and the idea that Atman and Brahman, the individual and the ultimate reality, are *one* is the essence of the Upanishads.

The basic recurring theme in Hindu mythology is the creation of the world by the self-sacrifice of God – 'sacrifice' in the original sense of 'making sacred' – whereby God becomes the world which, in the end, becomes again God." (Recall the cyclic nature of CGH)

The Cyclic God Hypothesis states that God created the physical universe out of loneliness. Being the only *Being* has to be lonely. And lest it be said that I am anthropomorphizing God, let me remind the reader that the Jewish and Christian Bibles state categorically that *we are made in God's image* (Genesis 1:26-27). The God of the Jewish Bible and the Christian Old Testament is clearly an entity with a full set of human emotions. Or, put more accurately, *we have a full set of Godly emotions.* So the motivation for creating the physical universe and all of the beings in it, throughout space and time, is to have *companionship.* This may be envisioned as a process whereby God *creates* all the finite beings of the universe, after first creating the physical backdrop within which these created beings will live, as is presented in the Bible (Genesis 1: 1-31). Remember, however, that God was said to have created Adam's physical body *and then breathed his spirit into that inanimate body* (Genesis 2:7). And in that scenario, we have the essence of the CGH concept of the Transcendent Godhead *infusing himself into the spacetime matrix.*

Thus we see the interrelationship of theopsychology and theophysics. It is a result of the psychology of God that we have the physics of God. God's mind gives rise to the intricacies of the spacetime matrix within the reality bubble of our entire universe. Galaxies, stars, planets, humans, and all the rest of this vast creation owe their existence to God's desire to have finite experiences which will assuage his loneliness.

What about the problem of evil? Since all of the focal manifestations are extrusions of the Immanent Godhead, then evil as well as good are experiences that God wishes to have. This is clear from the standpoint of the Atman/Brahman scenario, but it can be derived from the Judeo-Christian tradition as well. God is said to have created everything, including Satan. In the Old Testament, God utilizes Satan as an adversary for mankind. So, in Judaism and the Christian Old Testament, God evidences both good and evil tendencies. In the New Testament Satan is the personification of evil, and all evil everywhere is in some way connected to him. But Satan is God's creation, and the concept of a war between God and Satan, as though Satan and God are equal but opposite, is mistaken. The Creator cannot be at war with one of his creations, regardless of how powerful that created being is in relation to other created beings. Satan can make war on humankind, but never on God. If he thinks he is at war with God, then *he* is mistaken. God needs only to think him out of existence. So Satan, like us, is merely another way in which God can experience finitude through focal manifestation. Satan may in fact exist, and he may be able to tempt human beings into doing evil, but he is only another focal manifestation of the Immanent Godhead. I will leave it to the reader to think through the multitudinous ramifications of that. One obvious conclusion, however, is that Satan is simply another way in which God can experience his infinite potentialities within a finite space, and as such, he is useful to God. *God is as fascinated with evil as with good.*

And so we come to the end of our description of the essence of theophysics and theopsychology. I'm certain that the reader who has made it this far will have much to think about. Remember, *you are God's way of having a human experience.* Make that experience as fascinating as possible.

RECAPITULATION

I WOULD LIKE TO PROVIDE A brief summary of the critical elements of Scientific Panentheism, in order to differentiate my understanding of the topic from the numerous alternatives regarding panentheism discussed in the theological literature.

To the best of my knowledge, this system is unique in conceptualizing panentheism in both *general* and *special* forms. Technically speaking, General Scientific Panentheism (GSP) is the *meta-theology* (a theology about theologies), and, as such, it explains the nature and relationships of all basic theologies which comprise Special Scientific Panentheism. The *special* category is comprised of simple belief systems such as Christianity, Buddhism, Judaism, Islam, Scientism, Shamanism, Satanism, Wicca, etc. The Cyclic God Hypothesis explains God's nature as both unitive *and bi-modal,* in the sense that God is both Transcendent and Immanent, both *outside* and *inside* the material universe, and *cyclic* (in his Immanent mode), given that the material universe goes through cycles of expansion from the singularity and contraction to the singularity. God in his Transcendent mode is omniscient, omnipotent, and omnipresent. In his Immanent mode, God is *more* or *less* limited, depending upon the nature of the focal manifestation which he is experiencing. In Jesus, God had fewer limitations than when experiencing other human lives. As the Apostle Paul stated in his letter to the Colossians, "In Jesus the Anointed One, all the fullness of Deity lived in bodily form (Colossians 2:9)." Jesus was therefore a human focal manifestation without peer, certainly worthy of the term Son of God (uppercase), in terms of the intensity of his manifestation. And Paul also described the Immanent Godhead (Holy Spirit) in his diffuse form (as he flows through the spacetime matrix) *and* the Transcendent Godhead (the Father) in the following terms: *"In God, we live and move and have our being (Acts 17:28)."*

It is true, as we have seen in the course of my exposition of the Cyclic God Hypothesis, that mystics over the millennia (including some who were and are also highly accomplished scientists) have managed to become intensive focal manifestations of the Universal Mind or Consciousness. I will close this chapter with a quote from Nicholas of Cusa, a 15th century German philosopher, theologian, mathematician, astronomer, Catholic Cardinal, and mystic, whose description of his mystical experiences closely matches CGH, despite the differences in language which six centuries will necessarily create.

"I have attained the capability of experiencing my own essence within myself, and for me this experience becomes enlarged into another, *that in me and through me the universal essence expresses itself, or, in other words, knows itself. Now I can no longer feel myself to be a thing among things; I can only feel myself to be a form in which the universal essence has its life. At any moment I can have the higher experience that I am the form in which the universal essence looks upon itself. Then I myself am transformed from a thing among things into a form of the universal essence –* and within me the knowledge of things is changed into an utterance of the nature of things. *It is only in creating this higher cognition that man develops his nature, and only through the higher cognition of man does the nature of things come into existence.*" (Italics mine)

Nicholas of Cusa, *On Seeking God* (1452)

EPILOGUE

I HOPE YOU HAVE ENJOYED READING this book as much as I have enjoyed writing it. The main concepts have been swirling around in my brain for decades now, and it was time that I put them down on paper. Reading Dr. Fritjof Capra's book *The Tao of Physics* in 2002 helped to coalesce some of the ideas which were still a bit nebulous and helped to encourage me to put my ideas in writing. I thank Dr. Capra for motivating me to do what I'd wanted to do for some time.

Any defects in the concepts of the Cyclic God Hypothesis are strictly my responsibility. As I've mentioned in the Prologue, the outlines of CGH occurred to me in my late teens while a student at Cornell, and some components of the total hypothesis came to me during my pre-teen years. The details, however, were not filled in until much later when I started to read biographies of Einstein and books on physics for laypersons. I was unaware of the similarities between CGH and certain aspects of Hindu philosophy also until much later. But if CGH is correct, then it is only to be expected that numbers of focal manifestations, in this case human, would gain insight into the nature of the Transcendent Godhead and our place in his universe. *We are all One.*

I thank all of my readers for the time and energy you have put into reading this book in its entirety, and I wish you a life of continuing interest, exploration, and discovery. *Give to God the best life you can.* I have no doubt that he will appreciate your efforts. May the Spirit of God bless you.

- Dr. Michael F. Bohley, February 25th, 2013,
Prescott Valley, AZ

BIBLIOGRAPHY

Bartlett, R. (2007) Matrix Energetics. New York: Atria Books

Beck, A.T. (1976) Cognitive Therapy and the Emotional Disorders. New York: Penguin Books

Beck, A.T., Shaw, B.F., and Emery, G. (1979) Cognitive Therapy of Depression. New York: Guilford Press

Beck, A.T., Wright, F.D., Newman, C.F., and Liese, B.S. (1993) Cognitive Therapy of Substance Abuse. New York: Guilford Press

Braden, G. (2007) The Divine Matrix. California: Hay House

Brady, Jr., T. (1992) Thirsting for Wholeness. Florida: Health Communications

Capra, F. (1999) The Tao of Physics. Boston: Shambhala

Castaneda, C. (1998) The Teachings of Don Juan: A Yaqui Way of Knowledge. New York: Washington Square Press

Chilton, B. (2000) Rabbi Jesus. New York: Doubleday

Chilton, B. (2005) Rabbi Paul. New York: Doubleday

Freud, S. (1965) The Interpretation of Dreams. New York: HarperCollins

Isaacson, W. (2007) Einstein. New York: Simon and Schuster

Kaku, M. and Thompson, J. (1995) Beyond Einstein. New York: Doubleday

Lilly, J.C. (1972) The Center of the Cyclone. California: Ronin

Lilly, J.C. (1975) The Steersman. California: Ronin Publishing

Lipton, B. (2005) The Biology of Belief. California: Mountain of Love/Elite Books

McTaggart, L. (2002) The Field. New York: HarperCollins

Robinson, J. (1990) The Nag Hammadi Library. New York: HarperCollins

Ruiz, M. (1997) The Four Agreements. California: Amber-Allen

Sheldrake, R. (1995) A New Science of Life. Vermont: Park Street Press

Smolin, L. (2006) The Trouble with Physics. New York: Mariner Books

The Holy Bible, (NKJV), (1991). Tennessee: Thomas Nelson Publishers

Twerski, A.J. (1990) Addictive Thinking: Understanding Self-deception. Minnesota: Hazelden Foundation

Zukav, G. (2001) The Dancing Wu Li Masters. New York: HarperCollins

ABOUT THE AUTHOR

D R. MICHAEL BOHLEY IS A retired counselor. He holds national credentials as a Board Certified Christian Counselor, Board Certified Pastoral Counselor, and Certified Chemical Dependency Counselor. He is also an Ordained Chaplain. Dr. Bohley currently lives in Prescott Valley, Arizona.

NOTES

NOTES

NOTES

NOTES

INDEX

Islam 75

J

Jesus 12, 23, 45–52, 53–57, 59, 60, 63, 64, 66,
    76, 81

John C. Lilly v, 31

Judaism 72, 75

K

Knowledge xiv, xv, 7, 20, 26, 36, 75, 77, 81

L

Lesser fields 6

Light 16, 56, 60, 61

Lineage 36, 37

Luminous egg 39

Lynne McTaggart 29, 30, 35, 82

M

Machines 29

Manifest 11, 30

Matrix 2, 5–8, 11–15, 17, 19, 20, 21–23, 25–27,
    29, 31, 33, 34, 40, 43, 44, 49, 50, 59, 65,
    71, 72, 76, 81

Matrix Energetics 40, 81

Max Planck 6

Medium 14, 25, 30, 44

Messiah v, 12, 23, 46, 57, 59